PATHOLOGICAL

The True Story of Dating A Pathological Liar

To my family and friends, Thank you for always stick-
ing by my side and supporting me

To C.J.M., my heart always

Prologue

This is a true story. The names of the individuals involved have been changed to protect them. I was so invested in this relationship that I could not see what was so clearly sitting right in front of me. I was so vulnerable and desperate to find love. He was a predator and locked eyes on me, his prey. He is a sick, twisted individual and will get what is coming to him one day.

I hope this story is something that women can find relatable. I hope this encourages more women to share some horror stories of dating. I hope, if there are men reading, that you realize how difficult things are for women.

THE ONLINE STRUGGLE

Like any lady in her late 20s, I found myself online dating. It's the late 2010s. You don't just meet people in person as much anymore. I'm not in college anymore. I'm a healthcare professional with a busy and exhausting schedule. Everything is done online nowadays. Tired of seeing all of my friends in happy relationships, getting engaged and married, having babies, I decided to go back to online dating.

It had been about 2 years since I last used a dating app. I had tried two dating apps in the past. Plenty of Fish (POF) which is free and Match.com, which you have to pay for. From past experiences, I learned that there is very little difference in the men on either site. You would think that having to pay for Match.com would mean the men on there were more serious about settling down, getting married, and starting a family. WRONG! The messages for hookups, nothing serious right now, and dick pics came just as frequently from Match.com guys as from guys on the free site.

Not being willing to shell out that much money at that point in my life, I opted for the free dating site, POF. I signed up, being honest on my profile. Of course, the sharks smelled fresh blood in the water and pounced. I was flooded with messages. Ignoring the creepy "give me your number and I'll show you a good time" messages, I responded to the profiles that seemed like nice, clean cut guys. Some conversations didn't last past a few hours to a day. Others that lasted a few days but I would put an end to when the men let their true personalities slip out and tried to get sexual.

Being the ever pain in the ass that I am, I refused to exchange phone numbers with someone until we had chatted through the app for about a week. In my head, I felt this weeded out anyone with intentions to just hook up and move on. If they talked to me for a week on a dating app, that had to mean they were actually interested in getting to know me more. Or they were bored and didn't have an better options at the time. After about a week of chatting, we would exchange numbers.

Then of course, because I'm annoying, I would refuse to meet in person for at least a week. Now, I know what you are thinking, this lady is crazy. And yes, maybe I am, a little bit. But you can never be too safe. It did weed out a lot of men. In my woman logic, if a guy is willing to wait a week to get my number, a week to meet in person, then he must not be a crazy murderer or just looking for a hookup.

I'd been on a few first and second dates with guys. But nothing ever seemed to last longer than a few dates. There just wasn't a connection worth chasing after. I'm almost 30 at this point. I know what I want and need in my life and I know what I don't want or need. I'm not willing to settle down for just anyone.

FIRST CONTACT

It started off as simple as any other conversations.

A simple message, "Hey, you have a great smile and beautiful eyes. Hopefully we can get to know each other better."

He looked nice, clean, normal. AVERAGEJOE30. He was handsome. Dressed very nice in all of his profile pictures, sort of business casual. He lived in a town about 40 minutes away. His profile was a bit boring. It didn't give away any revealing information. He had a child. He was employed, didn't drink or do drugs, and had a car. Ok, I'll bite.

Some back and forth messaging, talking about our week, plans for the weekend. Enough with this superficial crap, I wanted to get more personal information. His name was Joe. He was a few years older than me, mid 30s. He was a financial consultant. He had a daughter whom he saw every other weekend. Was divorced for over 5 years. The conversation quickly shifted to me, my life, my hopes and dreams. Every answer I gave, he seemed to match up perfectly. This seemed to be too good to be true. Maybe I'm just overthinking things.

There was no push to exchange information. There was no push to meet up. There was just conversation. Easy flowing conversation the whole first day. This guy had potential.

THE FIRST WEEK

I would often wake up to a sweet message from him. Always calling me sweetheart, gorgeous. Always complimenting me on the simplest thing. He was always available to talk, no matter the time of day. He responded within minutes when I would send him a message. He made it clear very early into the conversation that he was not interested in speaking to anyone else. Wow! He's committed, dedicated. That's nice and refreshing. He's focusing on getting to know me. How many men are willing to stop talking to other women when you haven't even met yet?

He didn't seem to like talking about himself. But I continued to push. He originally was going to college to become a neurosurgeon. He had only been in school for about 2 years when his dad was diagnosed with prostate cancer and had to step away from the family business. Being the good son he was, he stepped up and ran the family business for a few years while his dad went through treatment and eventually decided to shut down the business. He then worked for the boys and girls club and worked his way through the ranks to also run that. He worked at the boys and girls club for years but then he decided he wanted to do something else with his life. That's when he decided to pursue a career in finance. He worked odd hours for a financial consultant. Going into work at 7 and being done work at 3. But what do I know, I work in healthcare.

He met his ex wife in college. It was a fast moving relationship. They married less than a year after meeting. They were together for years before they had daughter together. They seperated 6 months after their daughter's birth after he found her cheating on him. He was devastated. He was a loving husband and did everything he could for her. How could your heart not break for this man? Married for years, new parents. It was supposed to be the happiest time in your life. Only to come home from work and find your spouse cheating on you.

His parents were alive and living happily together in a retirement community. He had a half brother who had distanced himself from the family. He essentially grew up as an only child and that's why he wanted to have a lot of children.

He had been single for about a year, most recently broke off an engagement. She did not like to include his daughter in things they did, trips they were planning. He didn't like that so he ended things. Aw! A dedicated father who cares about his child and wants to be involved. Spent every other weekend with her, always doing some sort of activity. It's was such a nice glimpse into the kind of father he would be if we wound up together. Loving, sweet, attentive, active father. What more could you ask for?

Joe seemed to always want to talk about me. He wanted to get to know everything about me. I shared and shared. More often than not, getting a similar response or story. We were so alike in so many ways. We clicked on so many levels. It was so perfect. We had similar life experiences. We wanted the same things. This was great. This was so easy. There never seemed to be a lull in the conversation. Conversations flowed easily from one topic to another, from one story about our past to the next. Feelings started growing. It was more than just a crush. I really liked him. Maybe even more than liked him.

THE EXCHANGE

A week of online messaging flew by. We exchanged numbers. The texting and phone calls were constant. He was always
available for phone calls on my way to and from work. He was
able to text me constantly during the day. I loved the fact that
he was always so available to me. Always there to give me attention. I couldn't remember a relationship in my past where the guy
seemed to into me.

He was so supportive to me complaining about work. Lis-
tening to my stories. Always asking if I had any fun stories about
my day, if anything wild and crazy had happened. He wanted to
work in the medical field, he was going to be a surgeon. Medical
horror stories didn't gross him out like most people. He would
listen quietly as I sat there and complained nonstop about work.
He never tried to interrupt me or tried to give me a solution. He
was just supportive.

It was a whirlwind romance. We quickly turned to discussing our lives together. Discussing a future relationship. We
wanted to be committed to one another. We didn't want to talk
to anyone else. We both wanted to settle down, buy a house, get
married, start a family. We both agree to delete our dating profiles.

We started planning our first date. He wanted to plan
something super romantic. I wanted something simple, where
we could sit and talk. Really spend quality time together. He was
more than agreeable to go with what I wanted.

We spent hours discussing our likes and dislikes. Talking
about our pasts, what we wanted from our future. For every story

I shared about myself, he would have a similar story to tell.

As I drove to work one morning, we were talking on the phone. I had been complaining about not wanting to go into work anymore and how nice it would be to not have to work. "When we get married, you won't have to work."

"Oh I'm sorry, come again?" He was the first one to bring up marriage between us. We had talked about wanting to be married but not necessarily to each other. Hearing him say he wanted to marry me, gave me butterflies. No one had ever mentioned wanting to marry me before.

"When I was married to my ex, she didn't work. Once she got pregnant, she stayed home. So you would be able to do the same thing. I make way more money now."

"Ok. Well, we haven't met yet so you should maybe you should slow down."

Things continued to escalate over the following week. Conversations became more serious. Discussing love and marriage. Sharing pictures of engagement rings, wedding related things. Discussing timelines for the relationship. We both wanted to be engaged within a year or so. Married a year after getting engaged. We wanted a fall wedding. We picked out color themes. We would have children right away. We wanted 4 children. We already were saying "I love you" and we hadn't actually met yet. We were just meant to be.

"When you know something is right, you just know." He was always saying that. And it was just right between us. This was it for me. He was my forever.

THE FIRST DATE

Time came for the first date. We agreed to meet at a restaurant that was half way between our towns. Followed by a movie. Butterflies in my stomach, I got ready and started my drive. Figuring I would be early as was my usual M.O., I would be able to see him approaching, be able to get a good look at him before actually meeting him. I sent a text to give my ETA and he was already there.

I pulled into the parking lot and made my way into the restaurant. He met me at the front door. We exchanged hellos and a hug. He held the door open for me and we entered. We were seated at the table and began the awkward silent menu search. After placing our food orders, we began talking. He was so nervous. He was loud and talked a lot. I had to ask him a few times to lower his voice. He kept reaching across the table and touching my hand. It was so sweet and adorable. He was as outwardly nervous as I was internally.

Suddenly, two hostesses showed up at the table with a flower bouquet, gift bag and card. I turned 50 shades of red. I was beyond embarrassed. How sweet right? How many guys buy flowers and gift for a first date. Flowers, sure, maybe. But never a gift. It wasn't much. A little pillow with a kiss on it. And it smelt like him. He had put his cologne on it so that I could lay with the pillow and think of him.

Insistent that I read the card then and there, I obliged. It read

*I am so glad to have met you and been able to get to know you.
I can't wait to spend more time with you.*

Will you be my girlfriend?
I love you.
Love, Joe

Wow! Holy Moly! What am I supposed to do and say? I said yes of course. We had been talking about wanting to be in a relationship. We basically were already in a relationship. This only made things official. He was my boyfriend and I was his girlfriend.

Dinner went on pretty uneventful. Good conversation, lots of flirting. He complimented me constantly. When the check came, I reached for my wallet and he insisted on paying.

We drove over to the movie theater and got our seats. It was one of those dine in theaters. We looked over the menus. Without missing a beat, he ordered me a glass of moscato wine. My favorite. He remembered. I had only told him once. I blushed. We ordered a dessert to share and enjoyed the movie.

Following the movie, we sat in the car and talked for a little bit. Fun and easy conversations. He was just so easy to talk to. It was so easy to just start talking and opening up and telling things. He was such a great listener. He listened so attentively, always seemed to interested in everything I had to say, even the most boring things.

Neither of us wanted the night to end but unfortunately the time had come. He walked me over to my car. Holding my hand. He leaned in and gave me the most awkward hug and absolute worst kiss, no, worst peck of my life. I got in the car and drive home.

Once home, I sent a text saying that I had had a great time. Thanked him for dinner, the movie, and the treats during the movie. I teased that it had been an awkward kiss and hug and that I expected better next time.

The days following the first date flew by. The conversations continued. The planning of our lives together continued. Plans were made for more dates. Plans were made for trips we wanted to take together. He said he had a great surprise for a second date.

THE SECOND DATE

A few short days after the first day, came the second date. I drove to the mall we were due to meet at. I arrived early and waited for him. He showed up, so excited for the surprise that he had planned. He again had gifts for me. A candy bar and bottle of moscato.

We walked hand in hand through the mall. Looking in stores. Making small talk.

"What's the name of the place you work at?" He mumbled out something. "What did you say?" Another mumbled response. "I really can't hear what you are saying. Speak clearly."

"I work for a company that consults for Ameriprise."

"Was that so hard to say?"

He lead me through the mall to a small jewelry store. As we walked into the jewelry store, he was greeted by name. They knew him? He'd been here before? The clerk led us over to a case that contained rings that I had previously mentioned would be my ideal engagement ring but were way too expensive. I was ecstatic but also very hesitant. I had been looking at these rings for years. There's no way that he can afford these rings.

I got measured for my size and began to try on different rings. This was a dream come true. The rings were gorgeous. There was so many to pick from. Engagement ring shopping was something I never imagined would happen for me. He looked so excited to watch me try on rings.

We were then shown three different diamonds that he had previously picked out. Those babies were massive! How did he manage to do all of this? Why would he do all of this? This was only a second date. While I was questioning everything, I was beyond excited. No one had ever cared for me like this before.

We spent and hour or two, looking at rings, diamonds, and bands. This was all so surreal. Eventually I had picked out my ring, made the customizations that I wanted to it. The clerk took notes on everything that I said. I had never felt so special or important in my life. As we left, I asked him if he could afford the rings and diamond. He gave a cool and casual "Of course."

The rest of the date had to be changed because of weather. He had planned on picking up a pizza and having a picnic in a park. Unfortunately, it had started raining and was not going to let up anytime soon. He was so disappointed.

We sat in the food court of the mall and ate dinner. While we were sitting there, he brought up the topic of houses. He had been looking at houses for us. He wanted my opinion on location. We discussed ideal locations to live. Then he started showing me house listings that he had saved to his phone.

I almost choked on my salad when I saw the price. Quickly pushing the phone back at him, "I could never afford anything that expensive. I can't contribute to that."

"No, I told you, you would not be working. I would pay for everything."

"That house is a half a million dollars. You can afford a half a million dollar house on your own?"

"Yes, I told you that I make good money."

We continued to browse house listings as we finished our meals. I allowed myself to get lost in the fantasy. A big beautiful house. My dream kitchen. Everything I could ever want and more.

We walked to the car and drove to an arcade to play some games. We played arcade games for awhile. I allowed my super competitive side to slip out and he was just as competitive, if not more so. We battled it out over games. Making fun little bets for future dates.

Back in the car, we sat in the parking lot. Nervously, I asked him how much money he actually made a year and how much money he had. I told him that he did not have to tell me if he didn't want to. I know it was very early on in the relationship for this conversation to happen.

He gave a nervous chuckle. "You really want to know? You might not want to be with me if I tell you the truth."

"Yes. please tell me."

"I make $200,000 a year. I have $300,000 in my savings account right now as well as a few retirement accounts. I'll be able to retire in my 50s with all that I have in my accounts."

I felt my ears buzz and my stomach do flips. Never in my life had I imagined being around that sort of money. "You're lying."

"No, I'm not. This is why I didn't want to tell you. You don't believe me. You hate me."

"Chill out. I don't hate you. I'm shocked. I don't even have a portion of that in the bank." We continued talking about money for a bit longer and then changed topics.

I left that night absolutely dumbfounded. How does he have that much money? It was just beyond my realm of comprehension. I grew up in a small twin home, watching my parents work hard for every cent they earned. We lived a simple life. We never had extravagant things or took extravagant trips. I had my first job when I was a young teenager and never stopped working. I put myself through college and bought my own car without any help. To potentially be able to be with someone who would provide me such a life would be a dream come true.

THE HOUSE

A few more dates had passed, when he asked if I wanted to come over his house for a date night. "Of course, I would love to." He sent me the address a few days in advance. So I did what any other person would do. I hit up Google and stalked the house. It looked like a small house in a small little community off a major highway. Funny that a man with so much money lives in a small house.

The day came to head to his house. I pulled into the neighborhood and made my way down the roads until I came to his street. There weren't many people outside. But from the looks of the houses, it seemed like an older neighborhood. I arrived at his house and pulled into the driveway. The garden had dozens of gnomes, fairy statues, colorful rocks and even fake flowers. That's strange, he didn't seem like the type of guy to be into gnomes and fairies. Maybe he had them there because his daughter liked them.

I knocked on the door and waited for him to answer. I continued to stare at the garden, taking in the oddness of it all. The door opened and he greeted me with a smile. As I entered the house, the only thing I could think was *how can I manage to get pictures of this house so that I can show my girlfriends.*

Allow me paint a picture for you. Imagine walking into a home for old age people. Imagine what you grandmother's house looks like. There was a formal living room with large floral print sofas, coffee and side tables with lace doilies on them. Vases and baskets with fake flowers. Picture frames that were easily 60+

years old with photos probably the same age. Strange right? A small clock that chimes every 15 minutes.

The dining room had a large buffet with the "good china" and crystal stemware. The large dining room table had yet again another large vase with more fake flowers. The chairs had padded fabric seats, covered in plastic, covers with kitchen towels. Yes you read that right. Grandmother style!

The kitchen had outdated cabinets,counters, and appliances. Definitely had not had any updates done to it since it was built. All along the countertops were tons of little trinkets and statues. So many so that there was barely any countertop space to work on.

The family room had a small tv, maybe 19 inches. Another floral print couch with a recliner and an old pillow that seemed to be used as a booty cushion. There was a desk in the back corner of the room that was covered with piles of paperwork. In another corner there was a large bookcase. Next to the bookcase was a small table with an urn on it. I repeat an URN!

"Um, who's is in the urn?"

"The what?"

"The urn, right there is the corner. Who is in the urn?"

"Oh. That's my aunt."

"Your aunt? None of her siblings wanted her? None of her children wanted her? Her random nephew got her?"

"Yes."

There were children's toys in the corner belonging to his daughter. Another small coffee table with a large knit doily and a basket of fake flowers. On the walls hung printed artwork that was easily 20 to 30 years old. The artwork reminded me of art that my 80 year old grandmother used to have.

The bathroom also had not been updated at all since the house had been built and for some reason smelt like old people. Old people just have that distinct smell about them. Not a good or bad smell. Just the scent of old people. There were more fake flowers and trinkets in the bathroom.

There was a door that was closed. "What's behind that

door?"

"That's my daughter's room. And the dog is in there for now so she doesn't jump all over you."

The final room was his bedroom. A small twin sized bed, two large dressers and a bookcase. On the walls hung disney art and memorabilia.

"I have to ask. What is up with your house?"

"What's wrong with my house?"

"It looks like my grandparent's house used to look. The old floral sofas, the old print artwork, the tchotchkes, the urn. Worst of all the twin sized bed. I haven't had a twin sized bed since I was in middle school."

"I bought this house after my divorce. When I bought it, my parents were moving into their retirement community. They didn't need all the furniture so they gave it all to me."

"And you kept all the fake flowers and trinkets? And the covers on the chairs?"

"Yeah. I didn't know what else to do with it all."

"And why if you have so much money and make so much money, do you live in a house so small and outdated?"

"I didn't want to buy a big house and live in it all alone. I've been waiting to find the right person and then we would buy a house together. There was just always and answer for everything.

After a tour of the house, he had me sit down at the dining room table while he finished cooking up dinner. He presented me with roses. I was admiring and smelling the roses when I noticed something on one of the flowers. There was a green fuzzy patch on one of the roses. I began looking closer and there was mold on more than half of the flowers. Mold on roses. Something I had never seen before. I brought it to his attention. He did not seem surprised or phased at all by it.

Dinner was alright. Herb crusted chicken, oven roasted potatoes and broccoli. He was not the best cook ever. He said he usually had premade frozen meals rather than cooking fresh. This was surprising considering he said that his mother worked as a chef for years before retiring. Maybe she was too tired to cook once she got home so he never really learned to cook. We decided that he would not be doing much cooking once we lived together.

He had wanted to go out after dinner. He had bought tickets to see a movie and he wanted to get ice cream beforehand. I wanted to just stay in and have a nice night in. He was visibly disappointed but agreed. We spent the rest of the evening together watching a movie on tv, cuddled on the couch. As the movie was finishing up, he began dozing off. It was early, not even 9pm yet. He said that he had done a lot of house and yard work earlier and was just exhausted. He asked to end the evening early.

THE PROMISE RING

The topic of a promise ring had come up a lot in the first 2 to 3 weeks of dating. After looking at engagement rings, he wanted to get me something. We shared pictures back and forth of promise rings. That was also the topic of our first big fight.

He had been telling me for awhile that he had bought me a promise ring and that he was planning on giving it to me on a certain day. That day came and went. He said that he had wanted to meet my parents first before giving me the ring. I did not like that he had said he was going to give it to me and then just didn't. To me, that made him seem unreliable. He made a promise and did not keep it.

We had made plans to go to Olive Garden for dinner one night. He was again early. He had already gotten us a table but greeted me at the front door of the restaurant and lead me back to the table. Once sitting, we started talking about our days. He seemed distracted and kept looking around. Then he pulled out a gift bag.

Inside the gift bag was a small bag of Hershey kisses and a wrapped box. I began unwrapping the box. Inside the box was a cheap faux leather banded gold colored watch. I looked up at him and said, "Thanks but I don't wear watches."

He smirked and looked down at the table. He took the watch out of my hands and there was a small box wrapped with silver shiny paper. I picked up the small box, unwrapped it, inside was a beautiful, shiny ring. The stone was HUGE! Bigger than anything I had ever owned. He took the ring box from me and handed me back the watch.

"I stopped the time. Now you can look back at this watch and remember the day your life changed." He then grabbed my left hand and slipped the ring onto my finger. "It looks so beautiful on you."

Just then the waitress came back. "Congratulations! Did you just get engaged?"

"No! No. We didn't. It's just a gift." She took our orders and walked away. I felt bad for pouncing on her with my answer. This was insane. We had been together less than a month. This ring looked as if it cost more than I make in a month at work. I was so excited though to be able to show it off to all of my friends.

"I really hope this is not a real diamond."

"Of course it is."

"There is no way this was under $500 like you said you were going to spend."

"Don't worry about it. I have a jeweler. He gave me a good deal. Plus I told you that I can afford these things."

"Do I even want to know how big the stone is then?"

"It's a 1 carat diamond."

A one carat diamond? My one coworker had just gotten engaged to her boyfriend of 4 years and she didn't even get a one carat diamond. I didn't even want to begin how big of an engagement ring he was willing to buy. The thought alone made me sick to my stomach. I had never been around such wealth in my life. It made me uncomfortable because it was so far from what I was used to. But it also gave me joy and excitement. This was something I never in my wildest dreams could have imagined.

"Thank you so much. You really shouldn't have done this. This is way too much."

"You deserve it."

THE PROMOTION

As had become the tradition, I called Joe on my way home from work. He was rather chipper this evening. He asked me how my day had been, had anything wild or crazy happened. I talked, or rather complained about my day. It had become a regular topic of conversation, I wasn't going to work once we got married. I had become so in love with the idea of not having to work, that every-day I worked seemed to last forever.

When I asked him about his day he said, "Well I actually have good news. I got called into my boss's office today and I am going to be getting a promotion."

"That's great! What is your new position?"

"They are promoting me to CFO."

"Wait. What? Like for real? CFO? That's insane."

"Yeah. It won't be for a few weeks. I have to have a meeting with my boss again tomorrow to discuss the details of the job and the new responsibilities."

"Well that is just incredible. Congrats."

"And of course I will be getting a raise. will be making an extra couple of thousand of dollars a paycheck now. So this means that when we get engaged, you could leave your job if you wanted to."

I wanted to throw up. This man talked about money and the money he had like it was air or water. Like it was just some-thing that everyone had. It sort of bothered me in a sense. Not that he was constantly rubbing it in anyone's face. But just always sort of finding a way to mention that he had a lot of money on a regular basis. He knew that I did not come from money and that I did not have much money. That I struggled to pay the occasional bill.

"Well that's just great. I'm very happy for you."

"Well you should be happy for yourself too since we are going to get married. It will be your money too."

One day at work, a coworker had noticed the promise ring on my finger. She freaked out and started screaming. I quickly hushed her up and explained that it was only a promise ring. That we had been together for about a month. Of course, she wanted to know all about him.

I explained that we had met online and had been together for about a month. She had met her husband online and was married to him within a year. She understood the whirlwind romance and when you know, you just know. I told her that he was now a CFO for a financial consulting firm.

Being the ever suspicious woman that she is, she asked if I had called the firm and asked to speak with him. I said "No way, why would I do that?"

"Because you need to make sure that he is who he says he is. When I first met my husband and he told me where he worked, I called them the next day and asked to speak with him. When the receptionist said she would connect me with him, I hung up before I got connected to him. You can never be too careful. Give them a call tomorrow or I can call for you if you want."

"That's not a bad idea. You're crazy." And the thought never crossed my mind again.

MEETING MY PARENTS

One week after giving me the promise ring, we had plans for Joe to meet my parents. We planned to meeting at the same restaurant where we had our first date. As I walked into the restaurant with my parents in tow, he rose from a table in the back of the restaurant. He smiled wide and waved, excitedly.

As we approached the table we found two large bouquet of flowers for us. Next to the flowers was a large box. He walked around the table to pull out my mom's chair then ran over to our side of the table and pulled out my chair. Once we were all sitting, he presented the flowers to my mother and me. He pushed the large box to my dad.

"I wanted to get you a gift but wasn't sure what to get you. I've been told you love to cook."

My dad opened the box and found a rainbow knife set. "You really should not have done this."

"I love to give people gifts. I love seeing their faces light up when they get an unexpected gift."

We ordered our drinks and my parents began asking a million and a half questions. Did you ever notice how parents are able to hold an inquisition for a new boyfriend or girlfriend, yet it never really seems like it? It must be some magical gift you get when you become a parent.

It started out simple enough, talking about his parents, his daughter, where he grew up, went to school. Then the topic of his work came up. I was having a conversation with my mom while trying to simultaneously listen to Joe and my dad. I could have sworn that I heard Joe say that he worked for Ameriprise. I don't remember him telling me that he worked directly for Ameriprise but maybe I miss heard him the first time. He was mumbling after all.

He talked about his new promotion. How excited he was to be taking on a bigger role. How he had worked for this for years but never really thought this would happen. He had been a lead team member for awhile.

The rest of the dinner went fairly uneventfully. Everyone enjoyed their meals, Joe only ordered a shrimp appetizer for his meal. He claimed he was not that hungry. Joe treated us all to dinner, after all he could afford it now with his new promotion.

We said our goodbyes and my parents headed home. Joe said that he had a special place that he wanted to take me to. He pulled out his phone and typed an address into the GPS. During the car ride, he asked numerous times if I thought that my parents liked him. Did he make a good impression? Did he talk too much about himself?

He drove us into the city. The area began to look familiar. I come into the city every few months with my parents. We attend different events, have dinner, explore. He parks in a parking garage and we start walking.

"I knew we probably wouldn't have dessert after dinner. I was talking to a friend of mine and she recommended this great place in the city to get all sorts of chocolate desserts."

I had a feeling I knew where we were headed. When we got there, I didn't have the heart to tell him that this was a place that I had been to a dozen times. He was so excited that he was able to pull of a surprise.

We ordered hot chocolates and a chocolate fondue. The whole time we were having dessert, he was seeking reassurance that my parents liked him and that he had made a good impression. I grew tired of having to pump his ego and told him that I'm sure they liked him and I would talk to them the next day.

The next day, I was able to talk with my parents. They

felt he was nice, well dressed, clean cut. They were impressed with him and his career. He was doing very well for himself. We seemed very comfortable and happy together. They liked that he had treated everyone to dinner. It all seemed to be going perfectly.

THE FALL

It was a few hours before we were supposed to be going out on a date. We had made plans on where we were going. I was texting with a friend about how well things had been going between us. He had met my parents and they liked him. We were making plans for me to finally meet his parents and his daughter. Things were getting pretty serious between Joe and I. I was the happiest I had been in a long time. I saw a future with him.

Suddenly my phone rang. "Hey, what's up?"

"I'm freaking out! She fell at school. There's blood. I- I'm on my way to her."

"Wait a minute. Slow down and take a deep breath. What happened?"

"I just got a call from my daughter's school. They said she fell in the playground and hit her the back of her head. She cut it open and is bleeding. They can't get a hold of her mother. So I'm on my way. What am I supposed to do?"

"Did you talk to the school nurse? What did the nurse say?"

"She thinks that she is going to need stitches. But she's ok. She was upset but she's calmed down."

"Ok here's what you need to do. Call her pediatrician's office and tell them that she fell and hit her head. Ask them if you can bring her in and if they can suture it or if you need to bring her to an emergency room. You also need to calm yourself down before you get to her. You need to be calm and cool. You can't be panicking and freaking out. She's going to be sad and upset. You have to be strong."

"I'm just so upset. I'm worried about her and pissed off at my ex. How could she-"

"Stop it! She did not know that your daughter was going to fall and hurt herself. You don't know why she is unavailable. You need to relax and be nice. Your ex is going to be so upset once she calls and finds out what happened. You can't be mean. You have to work on having a better relationship with her."

"Ok I'll try. Let me call her doctor."

A few hours go by and I finally receive a text message with an update.

Joe: We are just leaving the doctor's office. They put a few stitches in and said it wasn't that bad. It's on the back of her head. So you won't ever see the scar unless she shaves her head. LOL. She apologized to me when I got to her. Isn't she cute? I talked to my ex. She's very upset she was unavailable. I'm going to take my daughter out to dinner and then take her home. I'll talk to you soon.

Me: I'm glad everything is ok. Have a good dinner. Talk later.

A few more hours had passed. I was laying in bed for the night. I had not received anymore texts. I sent a message asking if everything was ok, if he had made it home.

J: Yeah sorry babe. I just got home a little bit ago. I had to take the dog out for a walk and then I was going to text you. I had a good talk with my ex. She was very apologetic and upset that she didn't answer her phone. Everyone is fine though. Thanks for all your advice and help. I'm so sorry that I had to cancel tonight. I'll make it up to you.

M: No problem. I'm glad everything worked out. Talk tomorrow.

MEETING MY MOM'S FAMILY

It was Labor Day weekend. My aunt was having a family barbeque, as had become a tradition for our family. I invited Joe to come meet my extended family before the big winter holidays. Things were pretty serious at this point. Almost daily conversations about marriage and the future of our relationship. This was a laid back event with my family. A good opportunity for him to be able to meet everyone without the pressure of a big holiday.

He picked me up and we drove separately from my parents. On the drive, he mentioned that he had been speaking with his lawyer. "I added you and your parents to my will."

"What? Why would you do that?"

"Because, if anything were to happen to me, I want to make sure that you and you parents are taken care of. As well as my parents and daughter of course."

"You shouldn't have done that. We aren't even engaged. So many things could happen."

"I love you and I know that I want to spend the rest of my life with you. I want to make sure that you are set should something happen. I am worth a lot of money."

"Oh please. You can't be worth that much money."

"Between my retirement funds, bank accounts, properties and investments, I am worth roughly 15 million dollars. I made sure that your parents will get 2 million to help with retirement and anything they would need. And you will get 8 million."

Again I felt sick. I had to roll the car window down to get fresh air. My ears were buzzing, I couldn't hear anything else.

30

"You can't do that. You shouldn't do that. You should leave it to your daughter. I can't."

"Don't worry about it. Its done."

We got to my aunt's house and I began to introduce him to everyone. He quickly got drawn into conversations with various family members. I stepped back and gave him space, not wanting to seem like I was overbearing or eavesdropping. He bounced from person to person at the party. He was very comfortable and able to hold conversations on tons of different topics with each person he talked to.

Again it all seemed to be going great. He got along great with my parents and my extended family. He did not seem to have any problem fitting in. This couldn't get any better. There had been other boyfriends that I brought around to meet my family who would only talk to a few people or completely isolate themselves. Everyone seemed to enjoy talking to and spending time with him.

THE HOUSE SEARCH

We had been sharing links for houses since the second date. Discussing our list of needs and wants in a house. What our styles were. The links for the houses that he was sending were so far off from the house that he was currently living in. Polar opposite even. The houses he was sending were large and extravagant. They were clean and modern, newly upgraded kitchens and bathrooms. Nothing like the his 80s style house.

We discussed the current furnishings that he owned. It would not match a house with newly upgraded house. He agreed that all of it had to go. He said he was going to donate all of the furniture and decor to GoodWill or Purple Heart and purchase all new furniture for whatever house we decided to buy.

I had to have another discussion with him. I had no intention of putting my name on anything until after we were married. I did not want to be committed to a house if the relationship did not work out. We had only been dating for a month or two. You never know what can happen tomorrow. There was no way I could afford a house like the ones we had been looking at on my own.

I could not contribute to any house that we were looking at. He said that he had not expected me to contribute. He could handle any and all expenses. The only thing he wanted me to do was to use whatever I had saved up to pay off my student loans. He would give me access to all the bank accounts and everything after we got engaged.

We continued to share links to houses on a daily basis. One day, we had plans for him to pick me and go out to dinner. When he picked me up, he turned to me and said "I made us appointments to look at houses."

"What houses?"

"Two of the houses that we talked about. I thought we both really liked them so I made appointments. We're going to meet my realtor right now."

This came as a bit of a surprise to me. We hadn't really discussed seeing houses at this point. I thought we were just sharing house listings in jest. Looking to see the price, what was available, and to get a sense of our styles. "Wow. Really? OK."

We took the 30 minute drive to see the first house. We pulled into a small street with a cul de sac at the end. There were about 15 houses in the development. No other houses in sight. These houses were massive. I don't remember the listings that we had shared because I had not been serious about buying any of them. I pull up the listing for the house we were about to see. "You do realize that this house is over 600 thousand dollars, right?"

"Yes. I know. It's in my budget. And it's perfect for us. You are going to love it."

The realtor, Michael, pulled up and let us in the house. We walked into a large entryway and grand staircase. To the right was a doorway to the garage and a powder room. To the left was a formal living room that lead into the formal dining room.

The kitchen was my dream kitchen. White cabinets, grey countertops. Newly renovated with brand new appliances. A large island in the middle with bar seating. The kitchen was open into a small dining area and family room with a wall of built in cabinets and a gas fireplace. Off the kitchen was a split level deck overlooking a large backyard that backed up to woods.

Upstairs was a huge master bedroom with a large walk in closet. The master bathroom had blue cabinets and white countertops and white tile. A large soaking whirlpool tub and walk in shower with a separate room for the toilet. Three other good sized bedrooms, a classic looking hall bathroom and simple laundry room finished the upstairs. The basement had been newly renovated as well with a brand new full bathroom, wet bar, and 2 additional rooms that could be used for anything. There was 4 closets in the basement for storage purposes.

I was so in love with that house. I was sold. It was my dream home, everything that I had always hoped for and more. I didn't want or need to go see any other houses. This was my house. We made our way back into the kitchen. Michael was standing there waiting for us. "What did you guys think? Gorgeous, right?"

"I want to make an offer Michael. This house is perfect and she loves it. We don't want to go see the other listing. We want this house."

"That's great. Let's get started on some of the paperwork."

While they talked about paperwork, I continued to wander around the house. I imagined how I would decorate. Imagined the parties we would have, starting a family and raising my children here. This was going to be my forever house.

"Why don't we head down the road to my office and finish up the rest of the paperwork to get the offer in today. You could have an answer by the weekend."

"No. It's getting late and we have a reservation for dinner. I'll give you a call on Monday to set up a time to come over and finish everything."

Joe quickly ushered me out the door and into the car. We didn't have reservations for anything. We didn't even know where we were going to eat dinner. Why wouldn't he just want to get this done now so that no one else jumps on the house?

"Why don't we just go to his office so you can put in a offer? I don't mind waiting. I'm not hungry right now."

"Because it's going to take 3 to 4 hours of paperwork and legal stuff." I had never bought a house before. I was living with my parents. He had bought a few houses so he had to know what he was talking about.

We spent the rest of the night talking about the house. We

talked about paint colors, furniture, what we would use each room for. We planned everything. We started a Pinterest board for the house.

Over the course of the next few weeks, I continued to add to the Pinterest board. I would send links to different furniture or pictures of things I thought would be perfect. He told me numerous times that he was going to give me free reign over everything. That I could purchase anything that I wanted for the house. He would just give me money or pay off bills for anything I bought.

I finally told my parents that we had looked at a house and that he was in the process of purchasing it. His offer had been accepted. They had to go through inspection and make changes to a few things before they set a date for settlement but the house was his. My parents asked me to take them to look at the outside of the house.

They were over the moon. "This is amazing." Neither them nor I had ever imagined that I would ever live in a house like this. I was going to be living a fairytale life. This could not get any better.

CAUGHT IN A LIE

Less than a week had passed since telling my parents about the house. My dad came home from work. "We need to have a serious conversation." No conversation with my dad had ever ended well when he started out that way. "Mom has been questioning things about Joe. Some things just aren't adding up. He told one of your aunts that he worked for Ameriprise and another aunt heard him tell one of your cousins that he was independently working. Mom had me call a few different Ameriprise offices around where he lives and none of them knew who he was. She also looked up the house that he lives in and he doesn't own it. It says that his parents own it. You need to ask him the name of the place he works for. We have to get to the bottom of this."

I picked up my phone and sent him a text: What is the name of the company you work for again?

Joe: I work for a financial consultant firm that works for Ameriprise. Why?

Me: What is the name of the firm?

J: Why?

M: Cut the shit. Give me the name of the firm.

J: Diamond Financial.

I went to Google and look up the name. I sent him the address of a firm I found with a similar name.

J: Yeah that's it. Why are you asking?

M: You don't even know the exact name of the firm you work for? I'm asking because my parents have spent the whole day on the phone calling different Ameriprise offices, which you claimed to have worked for and no one know who you were. So why did you lie about your job?

While I was typing and sending this text, my dad was on the phone calling the firm he claimed to have worked for. He called twice. The secretary who answered did not know the name. Which is strange considering he was supposedly just promoted to be the CFO. The second call, she transferred him to the HR department. The person in HR searched all the records for anyone by his name and had no record of anyone ever working for them.

M: You better call me right now.

"I'm really busy at work right now, what's going on?"

"How about you tell me Joe? Why did we just call the Diamond firm and ask to speak with you and you don't work there."

"I- I'm really busy."

"No you are not too busy to have this conversation with me. So where do you work? This is the last chance that you are getting to tell me."

"I- I work in an office that I rent. I- I work independently. I'm a contractor for Diamond. That's probably why they don't know who I am in the office. Because I don't actually work in the office."

"That's odd. Why do you have to rent your own office? Everyone I know who is a contractor for a company actually works in the office that the are working for."

"Well I'm a - I'm an independent consultant. I do consultation work for them."

"If you are only a consultant and don't work for them, then how did you get promoted to CFO?"

"Well the CFO retired and they asked me to take on the responsibilities of CFO until they find a replacement."

"And how do you get paid? Do they send you a check or are you on their payroll?"

"Well it's complicated. You probably wouldn't understand it."

"How about you explain it to me."

"Well it's sort of like a payroll paycheck but it gets put into a card. It's just how i conduct my business."

"I don't understand why you lied."

"I didn't lie."

"But you did lie. You claimed to work for not one but two different companies. You weren't honest the multiple times that I or anyone else asked you what you do for work."

He began to cry. "Because I didn't want anyone to think that what I do isn't a good job. I make good money. I just work for myself."

The conversation ended shortly after the crying began. I had very little patience for the woe's me bullshit cry he was trying to pull off. I told him that he lied and he doesn't get to try to cry and make me feel bad for confronting him about it.

I explained everything he said to my dad. He left the room and made a phone call. He had called his brother who works in the finance industry. He wanted to see if what he was saying was making sense. My uncle said that it was possible that he worked for himself but he had reached out to a bunch of people that he knew and no one had heard of him. They couldn't find anything about him or his business online. Most independent financial consultants have websites to promote themselves. It was not exactly adding up.

The same day, as the job drama was winding down, I get a text from my aunt. She wanted to come over and talk to me. When she arrived, she wasn't quite her normal happy self. She wanted to get right down to business. "If I found something out about Joe, would you want me to tell you?"

"Of course I would. I don't care what it is. I want to know."

She led me to my room and had me pull out my computer. She went online and pulled up a page on Theknot.com. For those of you who don't know, The Knot is a wedding website that allows couples to create pages for their weddings. You can post the story of how you met, how you got engaged, information about your registries and wedding.

There on the page was Joe's face smiling at me with another woman. I searched through the page. There was no information other than a few pictures of the two of them and a date for the wedding. The date was a little over a year away. That's odd. I knew he had been engaged before. But he had made it seem like it was a year or two ago. Why is there a wedding page for a wedding date a year from now?

I thanked my aunt for bringing this to my attention and went to sit in my car. I had a phone call to make. I was furious and did not want my dad to hear me screaming or try to chime in on the conversation. The first call went to voicemail. "If you don't call me back immediately, you can just forget I ever existed." Less than a minute later, my phone rang.

"Who the hell is Sarah?" I didn't even give him a chance to say anything. He was so thrown off by the anger and hearing the name come out of my mouth.

"What- what are you talking about?"

"I'm not going to do this again. Who the hell is Sarah?"

"She was my ex fiance. What's going on?"

"Why is there a wedding website with pictures of the two of you and a wedding date for next October? Are you engaged? Am I the other woman? You have one chance to be honest."

"We never even started planning a wedding so I don't know why there's a website." As if on cue, the tears came.

"Don't you even try to cry and make me feel bad. You're the liar. You lied about your job and got caught. You can't be upset with anyone but yourself. I don't feel bad for you."

"That relationship has been over for at least a year. I didn't know about a wedding website. I'm sorry. Tell me how to shut down the site. What's the name of-"

"Go to hell. I'm not going to fix this or help you fix this. You can find this exactly how I found it and figure this out on your own. You are a grown as man. Handle you problems on your own. I swear, if I find out you lied about one more thing, I will destroy you."

After being confronted with all of the lies he told, my parents decided that he needed to have a sit down talk with them and explain himself. We set a time for everyone to sit down and meet. He came to house and walked in the door with his head down, not making eye contact, and tail between his legs like a dog who just pooped on the sofa.

"We aren't here to attack you or yell at you. We just want to know why you weren't honest." My dad was the first one to break the silence. "Why weren't you just upfront and honest from the beginning?"

"I didn't want to have you thinking that I struggled to make a living. And it can be complicated to explain to people who don't know finance."

"So you take the time to explain it to us and make us understand." My mom was furious. She had steam coming out of her ears.

"Why don't you have a website?" My dad was using the information my uncle had given him.

"That's not how I choose to promote myself. I have companies that I worked for in the past and they rehire me for new projects or recommend me to other companies. Word of mouth."

He sat there and calmly and thoroughly answered all questions thrown at him. He had an answer for everything. He stammered and got flustered a few times but it was written off as nerves.

THE BEGINNING OF THE BIGGEST LIE

It was a Friday at the end of September. I was going to meet Joe's parents for the first time the next day. After having cancelled the plans the first time, I was rather excited to finally meet them.

It had been an absolute horrendous shift at work. You know, one of those days where you are just barely keeping yourself together, where you have to hide in the bathroom for 5 minutes to just gather yourself and stop from crying. I was so ready for the day to be over, to be able to go home, shower and just go to sleep. Then came the text, "call home."

It was not uncommon to get these texts from my dad. Usually it was for something simple. So I called home. "Joe is here, he's very upset." He was speaking in a hushed, urgent tone. "His dad was just diagnosed with prostate cancer and he came to tell mom and me."

Here's my thought process and internal monologue: are you kidding me? He's at my parents house? Prostate cancer again? Impossible. Even if it is possible, it's not a terminal diagnosis. He's not dying. Why didn't he just call me? Why is he being so dramatic? This is annoying and not what I need.

"What do you mean he's at the house Dad? Why?"

"He said he didn't know where else to go and wanted to tell us in person. He doesn't want to bother you at work. He doesn't know that I'm talking to you. Can you come home early from work?"

"Come home early? Are you kidding me? Yeah, I'll just abandon my patients and coworkers to come home. No, I can't come home."

"Well what am I supposed to do?"

"Tell him you're sorry to hear about his dad and send him home."

"I can't just send him home. He's upset. He wants to tell you in person."

"I can't deal with this right now. I have to go back to work. I'll call on my way home."

So I go back to work, finish up what I need to do and wait for the next shift to come in. I began venting to a few coworkers. We all agreed this is just odd. Why would he show up unannounced at my parents house? Prostate cancer is not a death sentence. This is not something you are devastated about. Cancer is cancer and cancer fucking sucks. We can all agree about that. Most of my coworkers agree that is is strange but knowing me as well as they do, they tell me I need to be a bit more sympathetic.

So I call home again on my way home from work. My dad tells me that he's still there. I absolutely lose it. The tears that I've been holding back all day at work start to flow. The anger, frustration, stress, annoyance all come out. It's beyond frustrating to me that he's waiting at my parents house for me to come home from work to tell me that his dad has prostate cancer. I tried to tell my dad about my day at work but I get so upset that nothing coming out of my mouth sounds remotely like real words. He tells me to suck it up and get home and talk to him. Joe had mentioned to my parents that he was expecting me to call him on my way home from work as was the tradition.

So I hang up with my dad. Try to compose myself so that I'm able to speak and call Joe. He answers and seems rather chipper. I began to cry telling him about the horrible day that I've had, telling him how I was screamed and yelled at all day by family members, how I have other people's bodily fluids on my clothes. After I finish getting through how I just want to go home, shower and go to sleep, he says "Yeah, well, I haven't had the greatest day either."

"What happened?" Trying to sound as sympathetic as I possibly can given I know everything that he's about to tell me.

"My parents called me over to their house today to tell me that my dad has prostate cancer again."

"How does he have it again? Didn't he get his prostate removed the last time? I don't understand how you get prostate cancer again if you've already had it and gone through treatment the first time."

"Apparently he didn't get his prostate removed the first time."

Now this makes absolutely no sense to me. Working in healthcare if you get diagnosed with prostate cancer and you're going to pursue treatment for it you usually get your prostate removed. But yet again, trying to be a good sympathetic girlfriend like I've been told I need to be, I tell him "Everything is going to be okay. He'll get treatment and he'll be fine. Prostate cancer is more often than not not a terminal diagnosis." That he will be fine after treatment. I told him that we did not have to meet this weekend. That I understood if they wanted to cancel dinner so they could cope with the diagnosis. He was grateful that I cancelled.

He then proceeds to tell me that he's at my parents house because he wanted to tell them in person. He told me that he was going to wait until I got home from work but has decided that maybe he should leave seeing as I had a really bad day at work. I told him I knew that he'd been at the house for a few hours and I was not very happy with what he did and how he handled the situation. I told him that it was very overdramatic to show up unannounced. He told me he would go into the house say goodbye to my parents and leave.

We ended the phone call there and I continued on my drive home. I cried the entire rest of the ride home. I had just come off of the worst shift in my entire nursing career thus far. The verbal abuse, the workload was physically exhausting. My back was screaming for me to just lay down. I had been pushed to my limit. I could not handle anything else. I could not take on Joe's emotional needs at that moment. It was just too much on top of everything else in one day. I couldn't handle anymore.

As I pull onto our street I see his car sitting around the corner from my house. He's still here! Are you kidding me?! I now no longer feel bad for him and I am only angry that this is all happening right now.

I walk into the house through the basement and I can hear him in the living room talking to my mom. As I walk into the living room he turns and looks at me with a smile on his face. How can you smile if you're so 'devastated' that your dad was just diagnosed with prostate cancer? I think to myself. I sit down in the chair across the room from him because I can't even stand to be near him at this point.

"Why are you still here?" I asked.

"Your brother is going to be FaceTiming from California soon and he wanted to stay to see him and talk to him" my mom says. roll my eyes, knowing my brother, he's not going to care all that much to meet him. My brother calls, as if on cue, briefly speaks to him and says he's got to go.

My mom stands up and heads upstairs leaving the two of us in the living room alone. I look at him and say "I'm going to take a shower you need to go home. I'm sorry about your dad but this is just too much."

He turns to me and tries to hug me. I step back and open the door for him so he can leave. He says he'll text when he gets home and leaves.

Later that night, after I had a chance to shower and compose myself, I called Joe. "I'm sorry for how I handled things. You have no idea what I have been through today but that is not why I am calling you. I'm sorry that your dad has prostate cancer again. But he is going to be fine. He will see his doctor Monday and get his treatment plan. He's going to beat this again."

"Thanks babe."

"But there is one thing that really bothered me. It was very inappropriate for you to just show up at my parents house. You are in a relationship with me. You should have called me first and told me first. I am your girlfriend. We text constantly throughout the day. You know that I'm always available to you."

"I'm sorry. I was wrong. I didn't know what else to do."

"There is no need for you to go behind my back to talk to my parents. If there is something they need to know, I can and will inform them. You do not need to talk to them unless I am there."

"OK. I'm sorry."

We talked for a little bit longer. It seemed that he understood what I was trying to say. We ended things on good terms. He had calmed down about his dad's diagnosis.

THE HOSPITALIZATION

I had a vacation planned with my family for the middle of October. Joe was unsure he would be able to go because his dad was going to need surgery to remove the prostate. His dad would find out Monday when his surgery was.

Monday came and surgery was scheduled for the day after we were to get back from vacation. He was going to come on vacation. He needed the distraction.

The following weekend, I was again at work. I get a text message from Joe.

Please call me if you can.

"Whats going on?"

"I'm in the emergency room with my dad. I went to their house this morning for breakfast with my daughter and he was in a lot of pain. He also had been peeing blood for a few days."

"I'm sure he is fine. Let the doctors work him up and figure out what's going on. Keep me updated."

I go about my day, getting text updates, explaining medical jargon being thrown around by the doctors.

Joe: The doctors say that he has kidney stones.

Me: No. He would not be peeing as much blood as you say he was peeing with kidney stones.

Less than 5 minutes later, my phone rings. "He has a kidney infection and kidney stones. He is being admitted for antibiotics and will be having his surgery by Wednesday."

"What hospital is he at?"

After giving me information about what the plan is with his dad and the name of the hospital, he asks "Would you like me to call your parents and let them know what's happening?"

"No. I told you before that I will update my parents. There is no need for you to have any contact with my parents without me. I've already been updating them throughout the day. I can take care of it."

I get off the phone with him and send an update text to both my parents. Continuing on with my day, assuming that everything has been taken care of. A few hours later, an hour before my shift is done, another ominous CALL HOME text comes through.

"Are you sure that he said his father is at that hospital?"

"Yes, that's what he told me. Why?"

"We've called the hospital three times asking what room he was in. We even texted Joe and asked what his dad's full name was. There is no one in that hospital with any name resembling his name. Something isn't right. We wanted to send flowers to the hospital."

"I will call Joe and ask him what's up. I'll let you know."

I hang up. Wanting to hear with my own ears, I look up the hospital's phone number. "Good evening, How may I help you?"

"Hi, yes, I was hoping you could tell me what room John Jones is in please."

"Hold on for a second. I'm sorry miss but there is no one in this hospital by name."

"Could you please check in the ER. He was in the ER and is due to be admitted."

"Yes, hold on. No miss I'm sorry. There is no one in the hospital or ER with that name."

"Thank you, have a good night."

I hang up the phone. Take a deep breath. I feel my chest getting hot, my face getting red, anger rising inside me. I pick up my cell phone.

"Hey babe. What's up?"

"What hospital did you say your dad is at again?"

Confirming the hospital name only fuels my fire. "Then how come when my parents called and when I called, the hospital says that there is no one with his name in the hospital?"

The high pitched stammering began. "Well he was just discharged. My parents are on their way home."

"Why didn't you tell me that he was discharged? What happened to needing urgent surgery and antibiotics?"

"I don't know. My mom just called and said that they were being released."

"I can't talk anymore. I have to finish up at work."

I hung up the phone without saying anything more. Something was not right. None of this was adding up. None of this was making any sense. I got a heavy feeling in my stomach.

I finished up at work and got in my car. I called my parents. My dad answered the phone "So what did he say?"

"He said that his dad was discharged. I couldn't talk much so I have to call him and figure out what happened. I don't understand how he went from needing to be admitted for IV antibiotics and urgent surgery to being able to go home."

"Well he's been texting me and he's not making any sense."

"What? Are you kidding me? What has he been texting you?"

As my dad was trying to read me the text messages, his phone rang. It was Joe.

"Don't answer. I'm going to call him. I'll call you back."

I hang up with my dad and immediately dial Joe.

THE FINAL FIGHT

"Why are you calling my dad's phone?"

The high pitched stammering began. "Wha- what do you mean?"

"I was on the phone with my dad and he was going to read me the texts that you had been sending to him today and you called him. Why are you calling him?"

"I- I was going to give him an update about my dad."

"Are you dense? Do you just not hear me when I speak? Did I or did I not tell you that you are not to speak to my parents without me?"

"Well I- I just didn't know when you would be calling and I- I wanted to tell him.."

"Why was he discharged?"

"Well he is being transferred to the VA hospital on wednesday because that's where his surgeon is."

"So he was not discharged?"

"No he was discharged. He's at home with my mom now."

"So how was he discharged home and being transferred to the VA on wednesday? How is that possible? How come when my parents called the hospital earlier this afternoon when you told me that he was being admitted, the hospital said that he was not a patient?"

"Well some of the staff told him that because it wasn't a VA hospital that medicare would not pay for his hospital stay and he would get a bill. So he said that he wanted to be discharged. And when you are told you are being discharged, they take you out of the system."

"WOW! You must think that I am just to stupidest person

ever! First of all, if you need to be in the hospital for IV antibiotics and surgery, they are not just going to discharge you because you ask to be discharged. Second of all, a hospital can not discharge you with instructions to go to a different hospital. It's a federal law. Third, even if you are being discharged, until you physically leave the building, the hospital will be able to tell what room you are in. And lastly medicare part A, which everyone gets, for free mind you, at the age of 65 covers 100% of hospital expenses and stays. So lets try this again. Why are you lying to me??

"I- I'm- I'm not lying to you. I don't know what happened. That's what they told me. I- I-"

"Enough! You are lying. He was never in the hospital and I'm sure never even diagnosed with cancer. What kind of sick human being lies about their father having cancer?"

"I- I'm not lying. Why would I lie? Wha- What would I get from lying?"

"I don't know Joe. What kind of psychopath lies about their own father having cancer. What else did you lie about? Don't try to act like I don't know what I am talking about. I've worked in a hospital for 5 years. I've been a nurse for 8. I know how healthcare works."

"I- I'm not lying. I- I don't know. I- I-"

"I don't care anymore. I am done. Delete my information. Delete my parents information. Never contact me or my family again or I will call the police."

ATTEMPTED CLOSURE

I spent that entire night tossing and turning. Wondering if his dad did have cancer. What else did he lie about? What did he do for work? Does he have money? What else?

So I picked up the phone and made one last call.

"Hello?" A timid pathetic voice picked up.

"You have one last chance to tell me what else you lied about?"

"I-I-I didn't lie about anything. I called Michael this morning to tell him that I didn't want the house."

"I don't care if you buy the house or not at this point. I want to know, no, I deserve to know what else was a lie. Did you lie about your job? Do you even have money to afford a house that price?"

"No. I-I never lied about.."

"You know what, I don't want to hear about more. You very clearly have a problem. You don't know how to tell the truth. I don't want to hear from you again."

There was some stammering but I ended the call. And with that, went my hope of getting closure on the whole situation. Or so I thought...

CLOSURE AND
THE TRUTH

A few days had passed since I had ended the relationship. My days were consumed with thoughts and questions. What was a lie? Was anything the truth? Did he actually ever care for me? Was it all just a game to him? Constant questioning. Talking to my girlfriends about everything. Trying to make sense of everything that had happened.

I was sitting in the house, looking at my facebook page. I started searching. I found his ex wife's page and the ex fiance. Maybe I should message one of them. But he had made the ex wife out to be such a horrible person. Maybe what he said about her was true. He didn't talk much about the ex fiance. Maybe I should message her. Maybe she could give me some answers.

As I sat there contemplating what I would say if I messaged one of them, a thought popped into my head. The ring. He said the ring was a diamond with a white gold band. I could take it to a jeweler and have them look at it. Tell me what it was worth. Best case scenario, I could sell it and make a decent amount of money. The jeweler my dad used for almost everything had already closed for the day. I found another one that was open. I grabbed the ring and made my way to the store.

"Hi! How can I help you today?"

"Hi. I was given this ring. I was hoping you could look at it and tell me what the stones are and what metal it is."

"Sure, let me take a look. It's a beautiful ring." She walked away and examined the look. She was gone for a few minutes. When she came back, she had a sympathetic smile on her face.

"It's sterling silver with cubic zirconia stones."

"Thank you. Could you tell me how much you think it would retail for?"

"No more than $200. Is there anything else I can help you with?"

"No that's all. Thank you."

I walked to my car, holding the ring. Thinking about throwing it into the street. I got into my car and sent out a mass text to all of my friends. The texts poured in. Shock and disappointment. It was such a pretty ring with such sparkle to it. How could it possible be fake? Sitting there and looking at the ring, it didn't sparkle the way it once had. It was dull and dirty looking. It looked cheap. I drove home. What was my next move going to be.

It had been about a week since the break up. I was talking to my friend about whether or not I should message the ex fiance. She had just as many questions herself and wanted answers just as bad as me. She was going to send a message herself if only I would give her the girl's name. I decided that I needed to send the message myself. I wanted to get answers first hand if she even replied. I found Sarah on facebook and opened up a message. But what did I want to say?

Hi Sarah. You don't know me. But I am hoping you can help me. I recently got out of a relationship with a guy named Joe. I had found a wedding page for the two of you so I assume you were engaged. He told me that you guys were engaged and had broken up a year or so ago. Anyway, I want to know if the things he told me were a lie. He told me that he was a financial consultant and had been promoted to CFO. He told me that he owned a house. He took me to look at houses there were more than half a million dollars. He gave me a ring that he claimed was a diamond ring. I took it to a jeweler and it's all fake. I'm assuming that everything else is a lie. He did not own up to anything when I confronted him. I'm hoping you can give me some answers. He even went as far as to lie and tell me that his dad was sick and hospitalized with cancer. Hope I hear from you soon. I'm sorry to bother you.

I began checking my phone incessantly, hoping for a message back. Minutes turned to hours, hours turned to a day. Maybe she's working. Maybe she doesn't want to talk to me . Maybe she doesn't care. Maybe she doesn't use facebook anymore.

Two days had passed since I sent my message. Two long agonizing days. Nothing. No response at all. Had she even seen my message. I was beginning to lose hope that I would get a response at all. I had left my phone to charge for a while. When I got back to it, there was a message. But it wasn't from Sarah.

Hi, I just received a message from Sarah about a guy you used to date named Joe and your concerns about his lying. I am Joe's ex wife. I'll be blunt. He's a pathological liar. He cheated on me with another woman and stole my engagement ring WHILE WE WERE MARRIED to propose to her. He currently works at Shoprite and makes hot dogs. He got fired from the boys and girls club 3 years ago because he lied to his boss. He got fired from minute loan in June because he lied to his boss. I bet he also didn't tell you that he and I have a 5 year old daughter and he refuses to pay child support for her. I've taken him to court multiple times over it and he always gets out of it because he lies to the judge. I'll save you the wonder of what the extent of his lies were....everything he told you was a lie, plain and simple. His dad IS FINE. You dodged a bullet by dumping him. He's nothing but a deadbeat lying sack of shit. Sorry if I've come across as harsh, but after what he did to me, you would be too.

I was in utter shock. It was Amy, Joe's ex wife. Sarah must have forwarded my message to her. I didn't know what to say. But this was my chance. I had to get answers. I immediately responded and thanked her for messaging me. I didn't ask any questions. I didn't know if she was going to want to talk to me after the initial message. She sent an immediate reply asking what he had told me he did for a living.

M: At first he told me he was a financial consultant and then got promoted to cfo. When I confronted him about that because we could find no proof he worked for the company he claimed he worked for, he said he was an independent financial consultant. He told me that he gets your daughter every other weekend and was actually taking you to court to get more custody. He took me to look at a 650000 house he was going to buy for us. He told me he was in the process of buying it. He also took me to look at an engagement ring that cost 20000. He cried to me on the phone about his dad being diagnosed with prostate cancer. I ended things when I called the hospital and they said no one named John Jones was there.

A: Oh for crying out loud! His lies are escalating rapidly. Our custody agreement is that he gets our daughter every week-end but he CHOOSES to barely see her or call her.

M: I have to ask, he canceled a date because he told me that she had fallen at school and he had to pick her up to take her to the doctor to get stitches. Is that true?

A: NO WAY! She has never fallen at school, never had to get stitches. I can't believe he lied about his own daughter. Then again he lied about his father having cancer. I just spoke to his dad. He does not have cancer. He never even told his parents that he was dating anyone. He still lives with them. How long were you together? When did you start dating?

M: We started dating in June. We were only together for a few months.

A: You should know that he was still engaged to Sarah when you started dating him. He is a serial cheater. He has cheated on every single woman that he has ever been with. He moved in with the woman he cheated on me with. He cheated on her with Sarah. The other woman threw his things out onto the lawn when she found out. He was with Sarah for awhile and they were actually engaged. He usually gets bored with his relationships and starts cheating. He always gets caught. He isn't that bright. Did you get the med school lie as well?

M: He told me that he was in med school to be a surgeon

but had to switch majors so that he could run his father's business when he was diagnosed with cancer the first time. He told me that his parents were living in a retirement community.

A: Nope. All lies. He was never in med school. He graduated college with a liberal arts degree. His father never owned a business. His father is over 70 and still works 60+ hours a week because his mother retired when she was 50. They own their own house. He lives with them and doesn't pay any bills. He doesn't own a car or cellphone. He uses his mom's phone because he racked up thousands of dollars in overdue bills with Verizon and no one will give him a phone plan. He drives his mom's car. He can't afford a car of his own but even if he could, he was one in a impound lot and in our state, you can't buy a car if you have one unpaid for in a impound lot. I just saw him the other day at Shoprite. His shirt had stains all over it, his fly was down and his pants were hanging under his butt. I wouldn't be shocked if he got fired from there soon too.

M: This is just absolutely insane. I can't believe all of this. Thank you so much for messaging me. I wanted to message you weeks ago but he made you seem like a bad person. I was so convinced that we were going to be married. I wanted to message you so that we could have a good relationship. I wish I would have. This would have saved me so much wasted time and energy.

A: He wouldn't let you meet our daughter because he knew she would tell me and he thinks that I'm going to hunt you down and expose him. I figured he was in a relationship because that's when his own daughter becomes non important in his life. Do you know what it's like to have you child hysterical crying because her dad won't answer her calls or doesn't show up to pick her up? She will get to the point where she's like 14 and is going to tell him to F off because she's sick of his crap. When she was 4, she caught him in a lie and called him on it. And then wouldn't speak to him for 3 days. He always makes me seem like a horrible person so that the women won't contact me. He knows that if someone were to contact me, I would expose all of his lies. Not because I want to be vindictive but because I want to save women from being hurt and having their lives destroyed.

The conversation with Amy went on for days. I would share something that he told me that I was questioning. It was always a lie. She shared so many stories about things she had been through with him. It was mind blowing to realize that this man lied about literally every single thing he told me. There was not one shred of truth.

He is a pathological liar, a sociopath.

Made in the USA
Middletown, DE
18 January 2022

58996908R00035